The
Fun Book for

Christmas

Other Books by Melina Gerosa Bellows

The Fun Book for Couples

Wish

The Fun Book for Moms

The Fun Book for Girlfriends

The Fun Book for Christmas

New Ways to Have Fun
for the Holidays

Melina Gerosa Bellows

**Andrews McMeel
Publishing, LLC**

Kansas City · Sydney · London

For Chris and Mackenzie

ISBN-13: 978-0-7407-8581-8
ISBN-10: 0-7407-8581-8

Library of Congress Control Number: 2009926280

09 10 11 12 13 TWP 10 9 8 7 6 5 4 3 2 1

www.andrewsmcmeel.com

ATTENTION: SCHOOLS AND BUSINESSES
Andrews McMeel books are available at quantity discounts with bulk purchase for educational, business, or sales promotional use. For information, please write to: Special Sales Department, Andrews McMeel Publishing, LLC, 1130 Walnut Street, Kansas City, Missouri 64106.

Introduction

The magic of Christmas. In some ways, the joy of the season is a mirror, reflecting the essence of who we are each season.

When I was little, the **highlight of the year** was always Christmas Eve. We'd go to my grandparents' house for an Italian **family free-for-all.** One by one, each of us would sneak from the "kids' table" until we'd all wind up in the dining room with the adults, listening to them tell jokes and old family stories.

After dinner, **we'd eat homemade biscotti,** pizzelle, and struffoli. Several Sambucas later, an uncle would disappear from the table.

Soon **Santa made an entrance** to dole out the very toys
we wanted. (How did he know?!) If **Norman Rockwell**
had been **Italian,** he would have depicted the Gerosa
holiday scene.

It was only years later that I learned my grandmother had to take a
tranquilizer before we arrived. What was the **most wonderful day** of the
year for the **thirteen grandchildren** was a pressure-filled stress-fest for
poor Lolee. Christmas does not come one size fits all.

Over the years, **holiday fun** has shifted from getting presents to giv-
ing them. In high school, shopping for the **perfect gift for each friend**
and family member and wrapping each one like an art project provided
hours of **creative enjoyment.**

Later, in college, the **highlight** was coming home at the end of the
semester and reconnecting with **long-lost friends.** We'd all congregate in
the local bars as soon as possible to **catch up, drink draft beer, and flirt.**
Even **midnight Mass** was more for cute boy spotting than reveling in the
birth of Christ.

Living in **New York** in my twenties, Christmas was all about romance.
No December was complete without the **double date.** My best friend,

Karen, and I would always finagle a night to get **super spiffed up** in a new outfit, go to a fancy hotel bar (with a fireplace), and, on the arms of some **handsome gents,** wander around enjoying the **city decked out** in its holiday finest.

As I look back on all of those Christmases, it's as if a cast of different characters **played my part.** All of them had the **grandest time** and appreciated the **sights and delights** of the season. I never understood how people could hate the holidays.

Until the Christmas I found myself separated from my husband. I wished I could just **fast-forward to the middle of January.** Only then did I realize **how lucky** I'd been all those years. Holidays simply magnify what you're already feeling. If you're sad, lonely, or sick, of course they are going to be all the more painful.

Still, with two kids under five, I was determined not to let the doldrums ruin my **children's holiday.** Even if we wouldn't be the perfect family reading *'Twas the Night Before Christmas* in front of a **cozy fire,** I vowed to find some way to make this time **special for them.**

Sadly, I was several states away from the **Gerosa Christmas Eve bash** and would have to find fun **closer to home.**

Serendipitously, I got **an invitation** to the Christmas on the Potomac event at Gaylord National Resort, right outside Washington, D.C. Among its attractions were an **indoor snowfall,** a sixty-foot-tall glass Christmas tree, and a **water-and-light show.** I packed the **kids into the car** and hit the gas.

As we **wandered around** the decked-out atrium eating **gingerbread cookies** that we had decorated, part of me was **grateful** for a way to pass the afternoon. The other part, however, was feeling mighty sorry for myself. That year I got **coal in my stocking.** I saw an intact family walk by, and **tears filled my eyes.**

I desperately wanted to **go home,** but it was time for the **dancing water** and special effects show. Loud techno Christmas music rocked the house, and a fountain started shooting water up into the air, **illuminated by different colored lights.** The

water squirted higher and higher and higher, until it was a **breathtaking sixty feet up** and then splashed down all around us.

Two-year-old Mackenzie and four-year-old Chase **gaped in wonder. Watching their joy** ignited the light within me, and that's when I saw it, right there on the faces of my **soaking wet children.** The **spirit of Christmas!** My kids were happy. And this was a sign that I would find my way back to that place, too. It was the **best present** Santa could have ever delivered.

This book is meant to remind you that the **Christmas spirit** lurks everywhere. To heighten your awareness, these pages are **filled with ideas** to enjoy the pleasures of Christmas past, suggest a few **holiday treats** to put on your future **to-do list,** and, of course, to find some ways to appreciate the joy of **Christmas present,** whatever your circumstances.

Christmases are like **snowflakes:** No two are alike.

Each is beautiful and melts into a memory faster than you can download your digital camera. Yet year after year, the *season reminds me* that the magic is in each of our *reflections in my mirror,* always there inside us, waiting to be coaxed out with *a little fun.*

The
Fun Book for

Christmas

Host a party featuring Christmas pomegranate martinis.

Hire a piano player to come
play Christmas carols and show tunes.

POMEGRANATE MARTINIS

Serves 2

1 1/2 cups pomegranate juice
2 ounces Absolute Citron vodka or white tequila
1 ounce Cointreau, triple sec, or other orange-based liqueur
Cup of ice
Splash of sparkling water
Squeeze of lemon
Pomegranate fruit

Shake first 6 ingredients in shaker and serve in chilled martini glasses. Garnish with pomegranate fruit.

Put the "om" in home this Christmas by skipping
all of the events you dread, staying home,
and tuning into the spirit of Christmas present.
Play George Winston's *December*, light a candle,
and put your feet up.

Host a Brazilian New Year's Day party.
Decorate with white flowers and light blue candles,
and make wishes for the New Year to Yemanja,
the goddess of the sea.

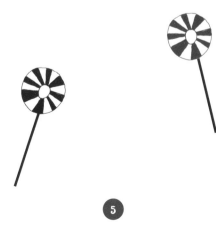

Deliver a tree, fully decorated,
to a family that can't afford one.

Make an annual event out of
watching *It's a Wonderful Life* and
The Christmas Story.

Choose a surprising theme—
such as a
Hawaiian luau—
for your Christmas Eve gathering.

Make a snow woman.

Give her all of the attributes you
wish you had. Drape her with a pine swag boa.

Start a tradition
where everyone in your family
exchanges crazy slippers.

When Christmas hits during
a serious transition (such as
after a breakup), feel free to skip
the holiday and head out for a
luxurious beach vacation instead.

Be green, creative, and inspiring
by using your little ones' artwork to wrap presents.

Sit and linger over a really decadent hot chocolate
at Godiva or Starbucks. Enjoy your own company
as you savor every single sip.

No matter what your current status,
make sure you get dressed up and go
on a romantic Christmas date.

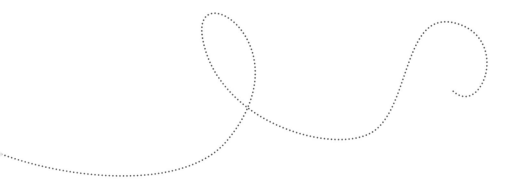

Celebrate the season with a family that celebrates
the holiday in a religion different from yours.

Make a gingerbread house.

GINGERBREAD HOUSE

One 12-ounce container ready-made vanilla frosting
1/4 teaspoon cream of tartar
Cardboard
Graham crackers
Assorted candy, pretzels, and cookies, including
   square caramels and shredded coconut

Frosting will hold each graham cracker building block together. To make the "glue," combine the frosting with the cream of tartar. To apply the frosting, squeeze it out of a sealed freezer bag with a hole cut in one corner.

To build the house, cut a piece of cardboard that's big enough to provide a base for the scene. Make the front and back walls out of whole graham crackers turned horizontally. For the two remaining sides, use a serrated knife to gently saw the top of a whole graham cracker into a peak. Run a bead of icing along the bottom edge and sides of the crackers. "Glue" them together in a rectangle on top of the cardboard. Prop up the walls while you work. For the peaked roof, run icing along the tops of the walls. Place 2 whole graham crackers, turned horizontally, on top of the sides, using icing to hold them in place. Let the icing set overnight.

For decorations, use icing and glue on your favorite treats to create doors, windows, trees, and anything else you can imagine. Let everything set overnight. Cover the cardboard base with shredded coconut to finish your snowy scene.

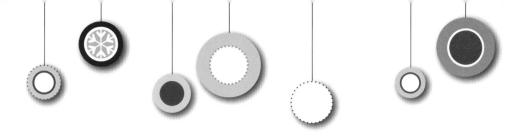

Decorate your house with nature.
Buy inexpensive white orchids
(at discount stores or the supermarket),
and tie red satin ribbons around them.
After Christmas, replace the red ribbon with
teal or orange for a fresh look.

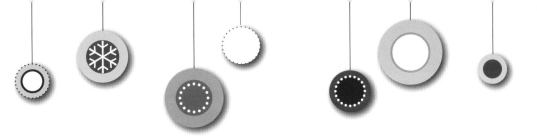

Host a hat party on New Year's Eve.
Give prizes in different categories.

Go ice-skating with the biggest bunch of friends you can gather.

Make sure everyone wipes out
at least once before the Zamboni
chases you off the rink.

Celebrate Christmas with faraway family two weeks later.

It'll be half the price, a quarter of the stress, and twice the fun as cramming to meet the December 25 deadline.

Celebrate the winter solstice on December 21.

Splurge on an organically grown herb wreath. (Enjoy the rosemary or bay leaves in your cooking all year long.) Cook an organic feast, including a cake decorated with a sun. Light red candles, and ring bells to usher in new blessings.

Have a truly green holiday by purchasing
a live, replantable Christmas tree.

Host an impromptu sushi-making party
the day after Christmas (when everyone is sick
of eating traditional holiday fare). Don't forget
the sake and the karaoke machine.

On Christmas Eve, pile everyone into the car
and drive through the neighborhood to see
all the different light displays and decorations.
Eat homemade popcorn and sip root beer
from a bottle with a straw.

Enjoy the scandal of letting your
best friends and siblings open gifts early.

Serve the traditional

Italian Night of the Seven Fishes Christmas Eve dinner.

Here are the courses:

GRILLED SHRIMP

. . . .

BAKED OYSTERS

. . . .

ROASTED SMELTS

. . . .

SMOKED TROUT

. . . .

GRILLED HALIBUT STEAKS WITH FRESH
TOMATO AND BASIL SAUCE

. . . .

WHOLE BASS STEAMED WITH ANCHOVIES AND CAPERS

. . . .

LOBSTER RISOTTO

Everyone gets dressed up.

Organize a
white elephant holiday grab bag
in your office.

The Rules

Everyone brings a gift worth less than twenty dollars. There must be the same number of gifts as participants. After drawing numbers from a hat, guest number one chooses a gift and unwraps it, and everyone admires it. On the next turn, guest number two can either steal number one's gift or choose any wrapped gift from the pile. If number two decides to take number one's gift, then number one must open another wrapped gift from the pile. On the third turn, guest number three gets to either steal any unwrapped gift (from number one or number two) or choose a wrapped gift from the pile.

Things to Remember

If a gift is stolen from you, you can steal someone else's gift or choose a wrapped one. The stealing continues until a wrapped gift is chosen. A gift cannot be immediately stolen back from the person who just stole it. The person who steals a gift for the fourth time gets to keep it. The gift cannot be stolen after that. The game is over when the last wrapped gift is opened.

Invite a bunch of kids over and spend an afternoon making tree ornaments

with bits of ribbon, found objects from the junk drawer, and materials from the craft shop. Praise each masterpiece for its creativity.

The first night everyone is in town, play Celebrity

(charades with pop culture references).
Serve cinnamon beef stew
with warm French bread for dipping.

CINNAMON BEEF STEW WITH PASTA OR RICE

2 tablespoons flour
1/4 teaspoon freshly ground pepper
2 pounds beef cut into cubes
Olive oil for browning
5 cups of water
1 1/2 cups rice wine, sake, or white wine
1/4 cup low-sodium soy sauce
1/4 cup sugar
8 scallions cut into 1-inch pieces
6 garlic cloves, minced
2 cinnamon sticks
1-inch piece of ginger sliced or minced
2 large portabella mushrooms, coarsely chopped, or button mushrooms halved (optional)
10 ounces of packaged baby spinach
1/2 pound of uncooked pasta or 1 1/2 cups of uncooked rice

Combine flour and pepper in a zip-top bag. Shake beef cubes in flour. Shake off excess flour. Heat olive oil in a Dutch oven over medium high heat, and brown the beef in two batches. Add more olive oil for the second batch.

Return all beef to pan. Add water, wine, and soy sauce to the hot pan and deglaze, scraping up the browned pieces. Add the sugar, scallions, garlic, cinnamon, ginger, and mushrooms. Simmer covered for 2 hours, or bake in oven at 275 degrees for 2 hours.

Meanwhile, cook pasta or rice according to package directions.

Just before serving, discard cinnamon sticks. Stir in spinach and cook until wilted, about 3 to 5 minutes.

Serve beef mixture over pasta or rice in a large, shallow soup bowl.

Swap houses with a family in a faraway land
to celebrate a holiday in another culture.

Christmas shop with your best friends
in a fun city on Columbus Day weekend.

Start a tree present tradition with
extended family members. Everyone draws a
name from a hat and sends three inexpensive,
small, extra-thoughtful wrapped presents to be hidden
in the tree and opened on Christmas Day.

Sit at the kids' table
at the family gathering.

Host a hangover brunch
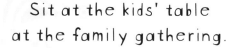
the morning after the biggest Christmas party.
Everyone comes in sweats and eats doughnuts.

Practice gratitude
the entire season.

Take an extra moment to look someone
in the eye and say thank you.

Strangers and loved ones alike
will appreciate not being taken for granted.

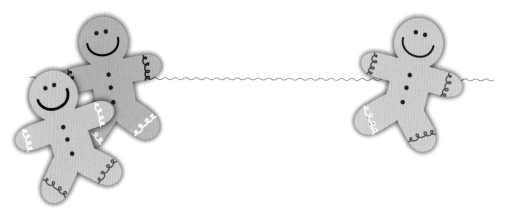

Do a conference call with your
best friends to discuss the best and worst
Christmas cards of the season.

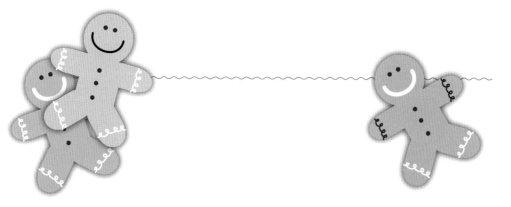

Host an intimate fondue party
the week between Christmas and New Year's.
Light a fire and serve lots of wine.

Bundle up the family and go for a nature walk on Christmas afternoon.

Everyone must go, Grandma included. Leave little treasures for each person to discover.

Give your friends experiences instead of presents.

Take them on a special ice-skating date,
or to museums, the opera, or a hookah bar,
whatever would be the most fun for them.

Go shopping with friends
for holiday shoes with bling.
Bonus points for feathers, gems,
and sequins.

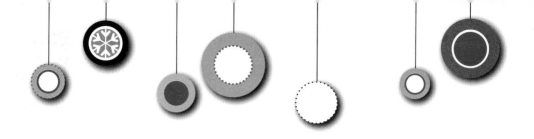

Give your
frequent-flier miles
to someone who really deserves them,
like your kid's special teacher, a faraway friend,
or a family member who could use a treat.

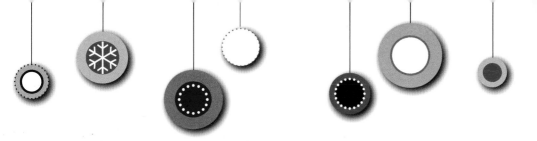

Listen to seasonal choral music

at your nearest cathedral or church.

Get a walking buddy.

Commit to walking every other morning
during December. Use the time
to discuss holiday parties, fashion disasters,
and New Year's resolutions.

Give a Christmas gift to your
least favorite body part.

Right after the holidays,
hit the sales
and hang on to the toys until next year
and donate them to charity.

Take kids to high tea
on New Year's Day.

Hang mistletoe (or wear it)
above places that
need to be kissed.

Buy a really good girdle
and look five pounds thinner
at your holiday parties.

Plan a Christmas date
with your lover.
Wear nothing but Santa hats.

Collect tree branches and put them
in a large glass vase. Attach Christmas cards
with bits of ribbon.

Have a fruitcake gift exchange luncheon.
Everyone brings the funniest gift
they've ever received.

P.S. Make sure everyone knows who is coming!

Have a "Shake It Off" party.

Invite your closest friends over for a potluck dinner the night before New Year's Eve. Everyone gets to share the year's worst. After dinner move out the furniture and dance like crazy to bring in new energy for the New Year.

Shovel a neighbor's sidewalk.

Make a friend a charm bracelet

with all the single earrings in your jewelry box.

Volunteer at a soup kitchen
Christmas Day.

Give your birds and squirrels their own Christmas

by decorating an outdoor tree with garlands of popcorn, birdseed ornaments, and cookie-cutter-shaped bread covered with peanut butter.

Fill his stocking with
everything naughty
and nothing nice.

Keep a glass jar in the kitchen and put in
the names of places where you and your
partner in crime have never been.
Christmas morning, take turns
picking the places you'll visit this year.

Skip work for a "snow day" and stay home.

Wear pajamas all day and make peppermint bark.

PEPPERMINT BARK

15 to 20 red-and-white peppermint candies
11-ounce bag of white chocolate chips
Red or green food coloring

Unwrap the mints and seal them inside a freezer bag. Crunch the mints by gently hitting them with a hammer. Remove larger pieces of candy from the bag and set aside. Pour the white chocolate chips into a bowl and microwave on 70 percent power for 2 to 3 minutes. Stir frequently until the chips are melted and smooth. Add the crushed mints from the bag. To create holiday color, slowly mix in drops of food coloring until you like the color. Line the cookie sheet with waxed paper and spread out the chocolate. Decorate with the larger mint pieces. Refrigerate for about an hour. Break the hardened chocolate into pieces. Wrap the candy in cellophane for a sweet holiday gift.

Arrange a coffee for your friends and their moms.
Let each mom share a favorite Christmas memory.

Throw a snowball at everyone on your Facebook page.

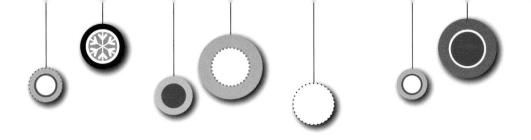

Christmas morning, feast on a French breakfast
in bed. Enjoy café au lait, warm croissants,
and fresh-squeezed juice.

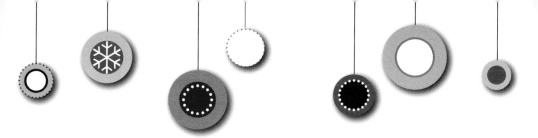

Send a care package to the troops.

Go Christmas caroling
with your friends
to a retirement community in the
ugliest Christmas sweaters you can find.

(Extra points for tacky hats and
battery-operated jewelry.)

Splurge on a delicious
cashmere scarf
that isn't red or green.

Host an Eggnog-off.

Everyone brings a different recipe
to see who makes it best.

EGGNOG

- 4 cups milk
- 1 teaspoon ground cinnamon
- 5 cloves, whole
- 2 1/2 teaspoons vanilla, divided use
- 1 3/4 cups sugar
- 12 egg yolks
- 4 cups cream
- 3 cups light rum
- 3/4 teaspoon ground nutmeg

In a saucepan over low heat, blend the milk, cinnamon, cloves, and 1/2 teaspoon vanilla. Keep stirring while the mixture heats. Remove from heat just before the boiling point. In a bowl, mix together the sugar and egg yolks. Make sure you whisk them well so they're light and fluffy. Gently pour in the milk mixture a little at a time while continuing to whisk. Transfer mixture back into your saucepan and heat over medium heat while continuing to stir. Keep stirring until your eggnog mixture starts to resemble custard. Never let the mixture reach the boiling point! Strain the mixture into a jug, making sure to remove the cloves. Refrigerate for an hour or two. Gently stir in the cream, rum, remaining vanilla, and nutmeg. Put back into the fridge overnight. Serve in cups with a little extra ground nutmeg, cinnamon, or baking cocoa sprinkled lightly on top.

Make trimming the tree a true event.

Take photos and keep them in a scrapbook so you can enjoy looking at years past. Make frozen hot chocolate.

FROZEN HOT CHOCOLATE

(Recipe created by Serendipity 3 restaurant.)

6 pieces (1/2 ounce) chocolate, a variety of your favorites
2 teaspoons store-bought hot chocolate mix
1 1/2 tablespoons sugar
1 1/2 cups milk, divided use
3 cups ice
Whipped cream
Chocolate shavings

Chop the chocolate into small pieces. Place it in the top of a double boiler over simmering water. Stir occasionally until melted. Add the hot chocolate mix and sugar. Stir until completely melted. Remove from heat and slowly add 1/2 cup of milk until smooth. Cool to room temperature.

In a blender, place the remaining cup of milk, the room-temperature chocolate mixture, and the ice. Blend on high speed until smooth, with the consistency of a frozen daiquiri. Pour into a giant goblet and top with whipped cream and chocolate shavings.

Find out what matters most to your friends

by doing a gift swap in which you all donate to one another's charities. See how creatively you can wrap the virtual gifts.

Have a Christmas Closet Clean Out.

Invite over your most honest and chic friend.
Model everything in your closet.
Package up the rejected fashions and deliver them
to a charity. Do the same for her.

Bring down the house by serving

flaming baked Alaska
for dessert on Christmas.

BAKED ALASKA

Serves 8 to 10

½ gallon (2 quarts) ice cream of your choice
One 9-inch or 10-inch baked layer sponge cake
8 egg whites, room temperature
⅛ teaspoon salt
½ teaspoon cream of tartar
1½ cups sifted powdered sugar
1½ teaspoons vanilla

Allow ice cream to stand until softened (not melted). Line a 2-quart ice cream mold or bowl with plastic wrap. Pack the softened ice cream into the mold, cover the top with plastic wrap, and freeze until firm. Place the layer cake on an oven-proof platter. Trim the edges of the cake to about 1/2 inch to 3/4 inch larger than the top of the ice cream mold. Invert the ice cream onto the cake, remove the plastic wrap (the plastic will make it easy to remove the ice cream from the mold or bowl), then return the construction to the freezer and freeze again until quite firm.

In a mixing bowl, beat the egg whites until foamy. Add the salt and cream of tartar and beat until soft peaks begin to form. Then add the sugar, one tablespoon or so at a time, until the egg whites are beaten to stiff peaks and all the sugar is incorporated. Beat in the vanilla. Reserve about one-third of the whipped egg whites (meringue) in a pastry bag with a star tip, if desired, for decoration. Spread the meringue over the frozen cake and ice cream, covering it well, so that it will not melt in the oven. Decorate with the reserved meringue in the pastry bag, or by making swirls and peaks with your spatula. Return the prepared dessert to the freezer until serving time.

To serve, preheat the oven to 450 degrees. Remove the Alaska from the freezer and place it in the oven for 2 to 3 minutes, just until the tips of the meringue have browned. Serve immediately. To flame the dessert (optional), after it has been removed from the oven, place a large sugar cube in the top center. Warm a tablespoon or two of brandy or rum until quite warm but not boiling, then spoon the warm liquor over the sugar cube, which will soak up most of the liquid. Hold a lighted match over the sugar cube until it ignites.

Organize your neighborhood to create a
landing strip for Santa on Christmas Eve.
Everyone puts out luminaries of
white paper bags containing candles set
in sand to light up the street.

Give yourself the gift of
not once thinking about calories
until after the holidays.

Have a quickie with Santa
(in costume, of course).

In the sleigh gets extra points.

Record all the holiday specials:
How the Grinch Stole Christmas,
A Charlie Brown Christmas,
The Year Without a Santa Claus, and so on.
Enjoy them with children or without.

Surprise your beloved
with a trip to witness the lighting of the
Rockefeller Center
Christmas Tree
in New York City.

Host a party
with a toy drive for kids
without gifts.

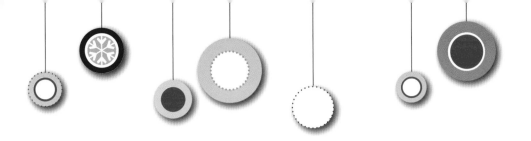

Read your kids
(or nieces and nephews)
'Twas the Night Before Christmas
every year.

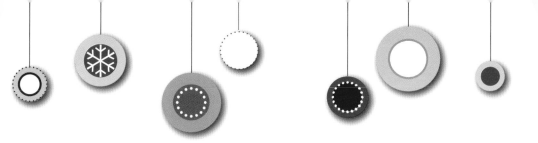

Get a Charlie Brown tree.

Celebrate nature's handiwork for the
unique treasure it is.

Go tandem sledding with a friend.

Scream as you race down the hill.

Arrange a Christmas cookie swap with neighbors or officemates.

Each person bakes their favorite recipe,
and everyone winds up with a tin
of different treats.

HOLIDAY LOLLIPOP COOKIES

1 cup shortening
½ cup white sugar
½ cup brown sugar
½ teaspoon vanilla
1 egg
2 cups flour
½ teaspoon baking soda
1 teaspoon cinnamon
½ teaspoon salt
Popsicle sticks
Colored sugar

Preheat oven to 350 degrees. Use an electric mixer to blend shortening and sugars together until smooth. Beat in the vanilla and egg. In a separate bowl, combine flour, baking soda, cinnamon, and salt. Then blend both mixtures together. Roll dough into 1½-inch balls. Push a Popsicle stick into the center of each ball. With sticks parallel to the cookie sheet, lay the balls 2 inches apart. Flatten each cookie slightly. Decorate with colored sugar. Bake 10 to 12 minutes, or until edges are golden brown. Cool completely, then wrap each cookie in cellophane or plastic wrap, and dress it up with a ribbon.

Make a party out of taking down the decorations before everyone leaves town. Provide lots of wine and snacks and add the video camera to prevent people from booking "early flights."